BREAK OUT

7 TIMELESS LESSONS FROM DROPOUT

BILLIONAIRES

Olaniyi King

BREAK OUT

7 Timeless Lessons from Dropout Billionaires

By
Olaniyi Ayeni

CONTENTS

Endorsement

I am quite impressed by the wonderful job that has been done in this book by Olaniyi Ayeni.

Going by the title of the book, I had traditionally thought that the points in this book will be the same as those famous, American motivational books in the market.

Truth be told, so many researches have been done on this topic. Hence, I thought, what could be new that can be taught about this subject? What a shock then to realise that this is an original book in its class. Each of the 7 points in this book is so practical, so unique, so original that I am, personally speaking, proud an African has done such a brilliant job.

Dear readers, please, if you are a business person or you want to be successful in any area of life's endeavour, give this book a serious consideration. I am especially impressed by chapter 2, "Dive in" Wow! This chapter will break off the chain that has been holding you back from daring. I want to congratulate everyone that will have the honour to read this book. Because sure enough, your success is imminent.

I also want to use this opportunity to appreciate Olaniyi Ayeni for taking the time and for going through the sacrifice of coming up with such a very practical and helpful book.

Kudos, more grace to your elbow.

Sunday Adelaja,
Founder, Senior Pastor, Embassy of God Church, Kiev, Ukraine

WHAT OTHER PEOPLE ARE SAYING

Breakout is a book at the eve of a revolution. It employs readers to be dent-leavers, seeking global approach to problems in the society rather than self-satisfying myopic pursuit. It asks us to break free from the norm and pursue our dreams with the desire not just to be wealthy but to create meaningful change and immense value.

Uka Eje.
CEO   Thrive   Agric

Break Out explores the concept of evolution to the point of man literally evolving, or for want of a better terminology, being 'born again', but this time into business, transforming from below average or mediocre, to something phenomenal, to a 'self-made' billionaire. It's inspiring and informative yet at the same time, the writer makes it clear that with the right structures in place, and the right frame of mind, the reader can achieve the status of a billionaire, not just financially but even as a state of intellect, increasing in knowledge and applying to the point of transformation. The journey starts by learning from those who have gone before. This book challenges the reader to be responsive to their dream before it becomes someone else's and encourages the reader that any dream is achievable. As you read it becomes clear that indeed the future belongs to those who dare to be bold and are willing to create it now; pursuing opportunities, and building platforms to reach their dreams. If you're looking for insightful tips and inspiration to achieve greatness and to progress on the financial ladder towards your dream, then this book is for you.

Debbie Akinkunle
CEO   Ministers   Desk

INTRODUCTION

The world is an evolutionary product of technology and innovation driven by people who have decided to leave a dent in the universe. They can be seen as the shapers and pace-setters of the world. Every decision they make affects every sphere of the economy; politically, socially or financially. Without them, the world may never have experienced such great advancement. They were once perceived as crazy and neglected by their colleagues and elites while starting out. They are the ones who defied the status-quo and now the "A students" work for them. I call them Drop Out Billionaires.

It might seem somewhat audacious to write a book about billionaires since I am neither a billionaire (perhaps not yet) or a Dropout. Nonetheless, I am fascinated and highly inflamed with curiosity about the lives of men and women who have amassed global wealth in their coffers and also made a significant contribution to the advancement of humanity in diverse fields.

The term Drop Out is commonly attached to people who left school before graduation. However, it also applies to people who left a regular 9 to 5 job in order to pursue their dreams.

Some of the personalities you will read about in this book are obviously admirable. But beyond admiration, I've come to know, both from my personal experience and others I've read about, that these men are not supernatural or gods in any sense. In other words, they came into this world the same way everyone did and were exposed to the same obstacles and challenges as everyone else –some even more than others. Their results can be reproduced by anyone; I believe –that includes you.

Brian Tracy once made a daring statement that, if we follow the same principles successful people follow, we would also have the same results irrespective of race, religion, nationality or background.

The world loves inspiration, but few love perspiration. When Thomas Edison said "*Success is 1% inspiration and 99% perspiration*", he sure knew what he meant. He knew the place of sweating things out. I live in a world far different from the world of my parents or grandparents for that matter and the changes in thought pattern have been dramatic in recent times. Much to my chagrin, I find that there are myriads of challenges facing the world. But *has there ever been a time challenges haven't invaded the comfort of man?*

I think not.

In the midst of the Holocaust, global economic recession, wars and threats of wars, unemployment and decay of the fabrics of society, these personalities have thrived and broken through. More like the tender plant that grows through the hard ground, they have emerged not only as positive stories to sell on the pages of magazines but as icons to be remembered even long after they are gone.

As one who has seen first-hand, the gap in the educational system and the real world, coupled with the prevalent ignorance, unpreparedness of youths in tackling the challenges of life, and the sluggishness to pounce on opportunities; this book addresses some of the wrong mindsets people have about chasing their dreams.

"I need to have a certification before I begin to work on my idea"

Does this sound like you?

Maybe not!

But it sure sounds like many people I've had conversations with. We often create mental limitations for the dreams we are capable of pursuing. If only we knew, in the words of Victor Hugo, *that no army in the world is strong enough to resist an idea whose time has come.* If only we knew, in the words of Steve Harris, *not to say NO to what our gifts can say YES to.* Then we'd have more people chasing and living their dreams, other than staying trapped in a mental prison of limitations that has no bearing in real life.

Sometimes, to chase the greatness we envision, we may need to drop out of a race that's not worth winning to start one that gives us the leverage to win and help others too.

With this, I welcome you to a journey to explore timeless lessons from the life of Dropout Billionaires.

I warn you,

Don't read for inspiration, read to find that which will help you perspire to greatness.

You are worth more.

Cheers!

Olaniyi Ayeni King

BEFORE YOU BEGIN THIS BOOK

This book will explore the lives of several billionaires. Notable among them are Bill Gates, Oprah Winfrey, Steve Jobs, Elon Musk, Mark Zuckerberg, amongst several others.

Those you learn from determine the kinds of result you have in your life.

I'm not only fascinated by their success, I'm inspired to be more, to aim higher and to explore every possibility to add as much value as they add to the world.

You also should aspire to the same ideals.

That's why I wrote this.

CHAPTER ONE

It all begins with a Dream

The biggest adventure you can take is to live the
life of your dreams.

- Oprah Winfrey

Ever heard of the term self-made billionaires? It had been a recurring word in many of the business literature I'd read. The meaning only became obvious –for the first time- while writing this chapter. Why are they called "Self-made?" I realised the term "self-made" is used for people who took themselves from nothing (or from a mediocre level) to become remarkable in life. It is the ability of an individual to transform his/her life from a failure to become a great success or celebrity. This isn't a feat that anyone reaches;

only a few have chosen that route and succeeded in it. Also, the term "self-made" reveals something amazing. It unfurls the possibility that one may be born more than once. One who is self-made went through a lot of transformational processes. Many self-made billionaires moved from nothing to billions. They practically evolved into who they are today.

Dreams have transformative power for those who choose to respond to its demands and not those who choose to be excited by it. A dream is so powerful that it could take a person from the humblest and modest of backgrounds to top the lists of the World's most influential people.

> *Many self-made billionaires moved from nothing to billions. They practically evolved into who they are today.*

As stated by Forbes, Bill Gates towers above several other billionaires and stands as the World's richest man. Considering his background, such feat provides a challenge to the upcoming generation to which I belong. Bill was born in Seattle Washington to a family of an attorney (his father) and a School teacher (his mother). Bill left his studies at Harvard University to pursue a dream that seemed unrealistic at that time. At the time, computer technology was in its infancy and those who were in the field were considered to be a geniuses and well-groomed for such tasks. But here was a school dropout with a drive to create a personal computer that would sit comfortably in every home. He realised this daring dream in 1975 when He founded Micro-Soft (Micro-Soft was an abbreviation for Microcomputer Software before it was called Microsoft).

Let me say here that dreams often seem unreasonable at first. A dream that doesn't dare you will not cause you to arise. People are not lazy. I think their dreams are only not strong enough to keep them awake or on the mill, grinding every single day.

A dream itself comes loaded with the very requirements needed for its success. The dream begins and continues to expand as it is worked on. Dreams come with demands which if responded to will bring about meaningful change.

Isn't it amazing how the Personal Computer (PC) has changed the world! This book in your hand (or on your device) was typed from a Personal Computer. Bill's dream came true after all, while he still breathes and lives on planet earth.

> *A dream itself comes loaded with the very requirements needed for its success.*

The power of a dream!

The only thing impossible is that which has not yet been conceived or dreamt of. Once an idea has arrived in the mind of a man, it means it is achievable no matter how difficult or against-the-odds the idea may be. Napoleon Hill captured this thought accurately when he said, "Whatever the mind can conceive and believe the mind can achieve." Written in 1937, his book *Think and Grow Rich* has sold over 20 million copies (at the time of his death.) As at 2015, the book had sold over 100 million copies worldwide, and has made several people billionaires with global success stories. His dream of writing the book is fulfilled when someone picks up the book to read, apply the principles and gets unquestionable results.

Dreams have transformative ability.

Bill's father, an Attorney, thought to allow his son keep on the trend of the legal profession – perhaps to carry on his legacy. While he was in Harvard to master the art of the legal profession, Bill took interest in coding, hacking and computer programming. His passion for computing increased till eventually, he dropped out of Harvard.

Opportunities are always present but only to those who dream and are willing to make it happen. Certain paths or opportunities in life will not open up until one conceives a dream. Every dream comes loaded with its own opportunity for fulfilment. Put differently, dreams create opportunities for the dreamer. While reading a magazine, *Popular Mechanics*, Bill came across Altair Computers Company. He called the company afterwards and told them he could build a computer program that could work well for their systems. Could he? Yes, he could. He had perfected his craft, working together with his partner, Paul Allen, to become better. But, had he built it by then? Not at all. He immediately got to work and *Beginner's all-purpose symbolic instruction code* (BASIC) was born. It was after the sale of this computer program that Microsoft was launched in 1975, co-founding it with Paul Allen.

This means that since opportunities are everywhere, the challenge is not the availability of opportunity but recognition of it. Several people must have read the same magazine Bill read but never saw an opportunity to create something. Perhaps, they didn't have the skill, or they didn't read that section. Whatever the case, when there is a dream in your heart, certain events and incidents would come to help in realizing your dream. A man with a dream carries a sense of detection which helps him recognise opportunities and seize them whenever and wherever.

Self-made billionaires have a greater sense of recognising and seizing opportunities.

It is amazing that Bill launched Microsoft after the sale of BASIC to Altair Computers. Could it be that the funds he raised provided the support to fund his own enterprise? He sold the BASIC software for $3000 to Altair Computers. Though he sold the software, he retained the copyrights. He could envisage the future.

A mentality of immediate gratification prevails in our time. If there was an equipment to checks the motives and drives of people who venture into business, we may find out that the making money is the domineering motive for venturing into business. In 2015, during a Summit in China, Bill Gates and Elon Musk were interviewed by another Chinese business Mogul Robin Li, Chairman and CEO of Baidu. One of the questions sent in was this: *"As a young man who intends to overtake you as the world's richest man, what kind of vision do I require and what specific advice will you give me?"* What is the aim here? Dollar signs are all over this question. The desire to be wealthy is not to be the pursuit, rather the pursuit should be the desire to create meaningful change and bring immense value to the world. Look at it this way, if you had a solution that costs just $1 and you sold it to 5 billion people today, you will become a billionaire almost overnight. But if you thought to beg people for that same amount or to cut corners to get it, it won't be as easy. It takes a simple dream and investing the required effort to make it happen.

> *Self-made billionaires have a greater sense of recognising and seizing opportunities.*

Making money isn't wrong or evil; rather it should be a means to an end and not the end in itself. Some people back out from their dream after making a considerable amount of money. Billionaires do not think that way. As a matter of fact, the mindset for value must be created from the start for it to stand the test of time, fame and money. Albert Einstein couldn't have thought better, when he said, *"Try not to be a man of success, rather be a man of value."* Those who chase the creation of value have success chasing them, pants down" (in the words of the Three Idiots). Much later, after Bill had built BASIC for Altair computers, IBM came to his doorstep asking him to build something for them. He bought 86-DOS software from Seattle Computer Products and reworked the entire system to meet the specifications of IBM. This was for the new range of Microsoft computers which was to hit the market at that time. Having worked on the software, it became MS-DOS, meaning Microsoft Disk Operating System. The point here is, Bill had foresight. He already foresaw the huge industry that technology will become many years later. He sold the software to IBM but retained copyrights and full ownership. His ability to have such a keen foresight was possible because he was not blinded by momentary success or financial reward he was to get. This is the kind of perspective we must adopt in order to create something tangible that would live on even after we die.

At this point, I'd like to say this – You don't have to start from ground zero to realise your dreams. You can find others who have attempted the same thing, leverage on what they have done and build your own success story. Being self-made does not mean being made *alone*. Like I stated earlier, Bill was able to find another computer company that had built the software he intended to build for IBM. He reached out to them, bought it, modified it and made it ready for deployment. Choosing to run alone can be detrimental to succeeding in life.

What happens when a Dream is born?

When a dream is conceived, there are always three kinds of people who come into one's life. The dream believers, dream builders, and dream neutralizers- those who would innocently antagonise the dream.

Don't Run Alone

Those who build dreams: Bill Gates had a Paul Allen to assist when starting out Microsoft in 1975. Steve Jobs had Steve Wozniak while starting out Apple. Google was founded by Larry Paige and Sergey Brin. Facebook started with Mark Zuckerberg, but he had other people who supported him. Dream builders help to translate a dream from being a lofty idea to something remarkable. If you need to seek out anyone in realising your dreams, they should be builders.

But how do you sieve them out of the large pack of friends and relationships in your life? The simple answer is to SHARE THE DREAM. Mark Zuckerberg, while sharing his story, mentioned that he invited seven people to the first meeting where he shared the idea of Facebook. One of his friends, Mr Green, chose to stay back in college rather than dropping out to work on Mark's dream. Obviously, he missed out on being part of the Billion Dollar Empire that was in the making.

Apart from Dream builders, there are those who simply believe in the dreams that we have. They are called Dream believers and lend their advice and counsel to you. This could be a Father or some respectable person who will be willing to share their life stories to spur you up and keep you going. We all need believers who will give us the needed inspiration to keep on going. It is great to have builders, but builders will only work in the direction and momentum generated by the leader. When the leader fails to give inspiration it affects the whole team. Dream believers fill this gap. Find those who believe in the dream and who edge you on as you succeed and even when you fail.

> *Dream builders help to translate a dream from being a lofty idea to something remarkable.*

There are those who are neutrals in this journey. They neither support nor attack the dream. Here's the wisdom: Not everyone is meant to be on your team.

There are those who at best should be spectators.

Dealing with challenges

Every dreamer will face big challenges at one point or another. Dreams are like fickle flames that burn on a candle. The fire must be protected in the open so it doesn't get quenched by violent winds. This is the same with dreams. When dreams are conceived, there will be criticisms and challenges, it takes the courageous dreamer to stay strong till the very end. In the life of billionaires, this shows up as numerous court cases and copyright infringements amongst others. History records legal resolutions between Microsoft and Apple Computers, Sun Microsystems, Netscape, Opera.

How does one respond to such difficult times? It is by being tougher.

In wrapping this chapter up, there are certain points I'd like to mention

- **Develop a Global mindset:** some global problems today threaten the very existence of humanity. In the last few decades, climate change has increasingly become a concern to every nation in the world. The records show that the heat and rays from the sun have increased at a very alarming. This singular factor has caused the glaciers and ice caps in the North Pole to melt. An increase of this will lead to rising sea levels, tsunamis and other natural disasters. Also, it is estimated that by 2050, the demand for food will increase by 60% and the world population will be 9 billion. Tackling this kind of problem requires a global approach and not individualistic pursuits. Self-made billionaires think globally. As a matter of fact, I think they reason like nations. This is why most of them own wealth more than the Gross Domestic Product (GDP) of several nations put together.

If you have a dream feed the world's poor and to never let a child suffer hunger, this daring dream could lead to the birth of an Agricultural company that mass produces food crops and sells at ridiculously cheap prices. Having a global mindset to an idea increases its worth, viability and sustainability. *Bill Gates wasn't thinking of the United States alone when he conceived the idea for Windows. He thought of the world.* The dream you conceive will either stretch you or limit you. I urge you to conceive dreams that will stretch you. For in that lies the ability to make you a phenomenal success. Think globally, dream with the universe in perspective.

- **Think beyond self:** In Third World countries, a part of which I am from, many are only satisfied with what they can get for themselves. This has resulted in a greedy life pattern. In my country Nigeria, tons of cash have been recovered from foreign banks; much of which was traced to the Late Gen. Sanni Abacha. He amassed the wealth of a whole nation to himself. Billionaires think beyond themselves. They have a dream to affect the lives of several others positively and not only to enrich their pocket. Today, there are several applications developed by Microsoft which makes computing very easy. From time to time, there are updates on the application to create a more convenient, friendly and effective interface. *Billionaires became so not by theft, but by a drive to be of service to others.*

- **Find a problem that you are passionate about, then solve it.** Not everyone will be passionate about ending greenhouse emissions or reducing the spread of terminal diseases. But when you look within you, there is something you would like to change. Mark Twain once said, *"There are two important days in life; the day you were born and the day you discover why you were born."* When you stumble upon a problem or challenge you are passionate about, it unleashes within you the capacity to provide a solution to it.

> *Dream builders help to translate a dream from being a lofty idea to something remarkable.*

✛ **Project into the future.** You need to ask yourself "What is possible for me?" By reading the trends, or simply thinking without the box, you can conceive an idea that could shape the future. To predict the future is to create it, *for the future belongs to those who discover opportunities long before they become reality.* Earlier I mentioned how Bill Gates had a keen foresight on the future of software and the possibility of sales. This knowledge informed his decision to keep ownership and copyrights to the software he sold to Altair Computers and IBM. He saw into the future and made changes. There is no better way to predict the future than to create it.

Never forget, in the words of Mark Zuckerberg, *"Dreams don't come out fully formed. You have to get started."*

Questions:

1. What is your dream? Get a note and describe it on paper. It doesn't have to sound perfect at first; it only has to be written. So, write it.

2. If you had all the resources in the world at your disposal, what kind of change will you like to see in the world?

3. If you had the means, what things will you like to bring an end to in your life, environment and the world?

CHAPTER TWO

DIVE IN

He who would search for pearls must dive below.

John Dryden

've never met anyone who doesn't have a dream. Really, there are two categories of people in life, the dream achievers and the dreamers. Since everyone has at least a dream, they can be called dreamers. But those who go further to realise their dreams are Dream Achievers. Sadly, there are only a few of them. If everyone who walked this planet had lived their dreams, we may only have a few challenges to contend with today.

So, what makes one achieve his dream while the other lives it only in the imagination realm? It is the Power of Execution –having a definite strategy to get the dream from thought to reality. The story I am about to share below would explain this further...

Defeating Hesitation

In a jungle lived a hunter and his little family. The man of the house had been a hunter from his youth; he mastered the art of getting the game from his father. He was undaunted and revered amongst the clan of hunters in the little community of the jungle. He was known to be fierce in the wild but tender and loving at home. As a medal of his bravery, he adorned the head of several wild animals all around the roof of his little mud hut. He was a hero to everyone including his family.

He would have considered himself a success, but for his only child who would not want to walk out in the day or in the night. He was born in the wild yet afraid of the wild. Neither the bravery of his father nor the persuasion of his mother could convince him enough to be brave and courageous.

The son has his heart in his mouth whenever the thought and talks about him taking after his father came up.

At times the father doubted if the son was his, but for the strong facial resemblance, he shelved that idea.

A conversation ensued with his mother one day. She asked, "Why are you so scared of the wild?" The son replied, "Mum, I don't know what is out there. I may get killed you know?" With a gentle tap on his shoulder, his mother said, "You are likely to die in this hut as you are when you enter the wild" His eyes flew open as she continued

"You are not to be afraid of the wild; there will always be danger every single day. You can't do anything about that. All you need is courage, bravery, and the heart to face whatever comes your way. With this, you would be able to stand firm even when confronted by a pride of lions."

The boy breathed heavily and tried to peep outside the hut to see the tall trees. It was evening and he could hear the sounds of animals a little distance from the house. He thought of what his mother said as he fell asleep.

He was awoken by noises and cries from his mother. In a moment, the hut where they lived was filled with people. Something had happened, he perceived, and it must have been really bad. He never thought it could be anything related to his father.

He looked out the gate and saw two well-built men carrying a badly wounded body which they laid in front of the house. They couldn't rescue him and covered him with a cloth because he was assumed dead. The boy who was still trying to come to terms with what was going on shoved his way through people and opened the cloth. He saw his father. His father who was struggling for breath, stretched his hand to touch his son's face and said "be brave, son. Be brave" and he breathed his last.

Then the cries increased for he had been a brave man indeed. A dirge and an ode were recited to celebrate his bravery.

The words of his father resonated in his heart as a surge of courage pierced through his soul. In that moment courage was born and his strength seemed to have been raised a thousand times more. He stepped out into the wild and got wilder than the wild.

He conquered not only his fear but became a hunter of a higher class than his father. Pride of Lions could not stop him, nor could the tingling sounds and steps of the strongest of bears deter him.

He dived into the jungle every day and everything around him was game.

What's the lesson in this story?

There are really no limitations in life. Whatever limits us from reaching forth to our greatness is most likely self-created. Your environment is not enough to stop you from living your dreams. Rather, it contains the resources for the success that you desire. Success begins on the inside. The fear within must first be conquered before stepping out into the *jungle for execution*. This does not mean there are no real dangers out there. But like a popular quote says, "a ship is safe in its harbour but it wasn't built to stay in the harbour. When there's no enemy within, the enemy without can do no harm" - Napoleon Hill.

One reason people do not dive into the execution of their ideas is because they allow excuses drown the bright light of their dream. Reading success stories and the biographies of billionaires are not enough; we need to read between the lines. Weighing between options in the pursuit of a dream is one of the biggest challenges that faces a dreamer.

In Africa, people excuse their negligence for studies and give well-crafted excuses for failure during examinations. Pointing at successful people who dropped out of school, they self-identify as success stories in the making –which they rarely become. To think that dropping out of school guarantees success is as ridiculous as thinking that wearing an expensive suit will get you a high paying job after an interview. Dropping out of school to pursue a dream happens when the dream becomes compelling enough to demand full focus and attention. No one becomes a success by dropping out, they become successful by paying the required price for it. So, if the price involves leaving school, go for it.

If you have an idea that gets you so excited, you will not only talk about it, you will do something about it.

Do you need the permission of anyone to succeed?

I developed a social formula a couple of years ago to prevent certain kind of opinions from getting to me. There are over 7 billion people on earth and each person has an opinion about a particular thing. Sometimes they have more than one opinion. Due to our closeness to certain people, we allow their words and opinions deter us from reaching the goal we set.

Why do we do this?

It is because we love relationships. We treasure family, friends and our different social groups. If you are going to emerge a success in life, you are going to have to lead your life (please read that last sentence again). You have to lead your own life.

No one becomes a success by dropping out, they become successful by paying the required price for it. So, if the price involves leaving school, go for it.

You have to be responsible for your own thoughts, decisions and actions. If the content that comes to you from those around you is unfavourable to the dream, then you've got to shelve it.

So, here is the idea.

When you want to start a business, for instance, and you share the idea with a friend or family, but they discourage you. Let's mathematically assume you received negative answers from 20 people in all.

Now,

Divide this number by the total number of people on earth:

Mathematically,

My idea = 20 negative responses from 20 people/ 7 billion people on earth

The answer in my calculator is 0.000000000285714285...

So it means you allow the opinion of less than 0.000000003% of the people on earth to prevent you from doing what you have always dreamt about.

From research, I understand that we need about 16 affirmative answers to cancel one negative opinion about us or the things that we intend to do. So, if 0.000000003% of the people on earth gave you a negative response, why not assume that the rest of the 99% on earth is in your support –raving for you?

You have to be responsible for your own thoughts, decisions and actions.

You may not need a reference

The fact that what you intend to create has not been created before doesn't mean it's not valid. We often seek examples, but you stand a great chance of succeeding if your idea is new and has the potential to solve problems for people. Back then in secondary school days, our mathematics textbook had examples we could use as a blueprint to answer questions in any given exercise. We noticed that the examples always differed from the exercises themselves. Many times, the examples were way simpler than the exercises. This tells me something, no two things are exactly the same. There is a measure of difference in everyone, no matter the level of similarities we may share.

> *The fact that what you intend to create has not been created before doesn't mean it's not valid.*

That's why you have to chart your own path when you do not find any. Robert Frost wrote a poem that clearly reveals the power our choices have in shaping our destiny. It is titled The Road Not Taken.

Ever heard about the Road not taken?

The Road not taken reveals how life really is.

Two roads diverged in a yellow wood,

And sorry I could not travel both

And be one traveller, long I stood

And looked down one as far as I could

To where it bent in the undergrowth;

Then took the other, as just as fair,

And having perhaps the better claim,

Because it was grassy and wanted wear;

Though as for that the passing there

Had worn them really about the same,

And both that morning equally lay

In leaves, no step had trodden black.

Oh, I kept the first for another day!

Yet knowing how way leads on to way,

I doubted if I should ever come back.

I shall be telling this with a sigh

Somewhere ages and ages hence:

Two roads diverged in a wood, and I—

I took the one less travelled by,

And that has made all the difference.

– The Road Not Taken

Written by Robert Frost

Aren't we like this? We want to be like our friends, our relatives or some super hero or celebrity on TV. You can chart your own path; they created a unique path for themselves. Like that boy, don't be afraid to go into the wild.

Being decisive is at the root of diving into your dream. Our destinies begin to take shape at the point of making decisions.

The Man with a thousand Patents

"I'm an inventor. I can't be told what to do. I've got to do the things I want to do. I work with ideas, visionary things. Nobody—not even I— knows how useful they're going to be or how profitable until I had a chance to work them out in my own way."

These words were from a man born into a middle-income family in the 19th century. Much early in life, he had hearing difficulties due to a fever and other related issues. Having only three months of formal schooling, he dropped out, or in proper terms, his mother dropped him out of school. His teachers could not stand his level of curiosity and inquiry into how everything worked. His questions and penchant to know more soon wore his teachers out. They began to make comparisons between him and his contemporaries in a discouraging way. His mother knew better and labelled his behaviour as a mark of unique intelligence, he was a genius she would say. Truly, he was. In time, he rose to become one of the finest investors the world has. There were over a thousand patents to his name at his death. This man was Thomas Edison. Though he is well known for his incandescent light bulb, there are several other inventions tied to his name but not completed as at the time of his death. Edison was a practical example of a kid who dived in. It was said that he was fascinated by almost everything.

Whenever he saw something working, he would ask his parents or anyone around him why it worked. He wanted to understand the mechanics of how things were built and how they operated.

Truly, he needed education, but not the type that the educational system of his time offered. He opted out for being self-taught. His parents bought books which he devoured voraciously. Soon enough, his parents registered him in a public library to read books where he schooled himself and his appetite for the sciences grew.

A few more years and he would begin to invent things that would change the world. Of repute was the invention of the light bulb which history records was a product of over 9000 attempts. At the end, he had learned over 9000 ways not to create the light bulb.

Thomas Edison was a dive-in fellow. He didn't feel limited by his three meagre months of schooling. He knew where to get what he needed and he went after it. He asked questions from those around him and dived into creating whatever he envisioned in mind.

Here is the point

Whatever is worth doing is worth doing badly at first. Why? Because it can be improved upon as time goes on. The key word here is MAKE ATTEMPT. Take a plunge. Greatness is not only in the details; it is in the execution. Edison did not tinker around with his ideas. He dived in by asking questions and failing over and over again till he got it right.

From this, we can understand that much of success is 1% inspiration and, 99% perspiration. It is not enough to be inspired by an idea; at least most people get inspired. Mental toughness is needed to translate that idea into something tangible. The result is always greater than the idea.

What diving in is not...

Diving in is not a hasty generalisation. Diving in does not mean being careless with your finances or investment. Diving in does not mean being irresponsible with your choices and decisions. And it definitely does not mean taking uncalculated risks.

There are stories I've read that never cease to amuse me about the kinds of unnecessary risks people take with their lives –risks which are informed by ignorance rather than knowledge. People dive into things they have little knowledge about and wonder why they never make headway.

> It is not enough to be inspired by an idea; at least most people get inspired.

To digress a bit from wealth and success, I'd share a story of a man known to be a prophet who decided to be friends with the lions for a day to prove how great his God was. "Inspired" by the story of Daniel in the scriptures, he also thought to repeat the same feat. In this case, no one sentenced him to such damnation; he sentenced himself. Unfortunately, unlike his inspiration – Daniel, there was no angel to seal the mouths of the lions. The Lions gave him a surprised look and in no time, the bellies of the lions became his new home. There are countless experiences similar to this. Though this example seems far-fetched, yet it has a lot of lessons for us as regards what diving in is not.

Don't try to live another person's dream and expect to succeed- the best you will amount to is a mediocre that would soon fade from the scene. The prophet in the story tried to live the story of Daniel. Rather than becoming the hero that Daniel rose to become, he became a lesson for others –a bad one at that. He is a perfect example of a person who takes action without understanding the requirements needed to succeed at it.

If you are going to succeed in your venture, or build a business, then you have to get your facts right. Understand your "why" for doing it. Your "why" will keep you going long after the prior motivation has left.

How to dive in

Many times we know what to do, but how to do it becomes one of the biggest problems we face. Billionaires we've examined and will still examine are people who understand the art of execution. It is better to be an execution addict than to be an idea junkie. Here are some steps to take to take that dive.

Develop the mindset for it: Just like the wall clock, the mind can also be set to function in a certain way. The mind can be trained and developed just like every other part of the body can be trained and developed. The first step to greatness is not trying to do things but developing the mindset that will give birth to those results. The great and the very successful understand that an idea in hand is better than an idea in the head. So, their mindset is programmed in such a way that as soon as the ideas land into their consciousness, they begin to paint a project in their head and begin mapping out the plan for execution. Once the idea can be easily comprehended in the confines of the mind, it becomes easy to communicate it and to translate it into workable actions which can be measured over time. The mindset is the most important factor in achieving success here.

Quick Exercise:

What one idea do you have now that you will like to execute?

Steve Jobs, Mark Zuckerberg, Bill Gates, all left school in the pursuit of their ideas and dreams. They developed a certain mindset that made them tough to face the real world rather than staying safe in school to pursue things that would not have brought the kind of change that we see in the world today. The mind is the home of your thoughts. Having a great mind means having great thoughts – the sum total of our thoughts and mental patterns constitute our mindset and how we react and respond to things. So, what should your mind contain, or how does the mind of a billionaire function?

> *You must have the mindset that your dream is possible and that it will have a positive impact on people's lives.*

They do not think of failure as others do: There is a difference between failure and feedback. Great people view the roadblocks they meet as feedback. They have a strong belief in their dream and know it is worth pursuing at whatever cost. You must have the mindset that your dream is possible and that it will have a positive impact on people's lives. It may not be global, but right where you are, the dream that burns within you could take the world by storm. You may not have the dream to build a TESLA or a COCA- COLA bottling company, but you could create a social enterprise or small business that would impact your immediate community and the world. And today, with the rise of the digital revolution, you can affect the world from your very location. Billionaires think BIG. There is very little difference between billionaires and their big thinking -they go hand in hand. While several people are contented with getting by with life – having a job, having a small family, saving for retirement and living a good old age, billionaires are busy creating massive wealth, engaging in heartfelt philanthropy and attacking diseases that threaten the existence of the human race. They have daring dreams and this is what keeps them motivated to strive for more, despite the perception that they have more than enough already.

Another thing about this mindset is responsibility. A lot of people believe that their success or wealth is tied to someone else. People blame their background, parents, economy and anything possible to excuse their failure and weakness to take initiative. It takes having a different perception to alter preconceived notions of people and pursue the dream you have in your heart.

Place a demand on your initiative and intelligence:

Taking initiative has nothing to do with taking an IQ test. You do not need an IQ test to prove the extent of your intelligence. Everyone is intelligent. It's been said that if Albert Einstein were born in our times, he would have been called uneducable and labelled as having Attention Deficit Disorder (ADD). This would have relegated him to the background and he would have amounted to nothing in life. He was said to have been particularly very active in class.

Today, when you pick up a cell phone you are engaging a theory that formulated by him.

The fundamental of physics that he figured out underpins much of our modern day life. His theories brought about the invention of lasers, telecommunication satellites, even nuclear energy.

Albert Einstein placed a demand on his intelligence. He did not need the school system to validate his level of intelligence before he gave birth to his ideas. His validation was within himself. With the power of imagination and deep thinking, he was able to unravel discoveries that amaze scientists. This formed the bedrock of most of the technology we now use.

The goal should be to create something that can add value to a

> *billion people consistently; money*
> *will flow in without stress.*

Becoming a billionaire is only a side effect of the principles that are discussed in this book. The real goal is how you can influence your world. Making a billion is not and should never be the goal. The goal should be to create something that can add value to a billion people consistently; money will flow in without stress. Placing demand on creativity and intelligence brought about Microsoft as discussed earlier. It is responsible for the break out of Facebook and several other successful companies and individuals in the world.

Take initiative to document your idea –do something each day in the advancement of your dream. Your intelligence is not about being great with numbers; it's being able to turn what is available around you into what is desirable.

I found the story of The Boy who harnessed the power of the Wind quite interesting. It is one of the most intriguing stories I've ever read about. Here was William Kamkwanba who was born in one of the poor communities in Malawi. His family lived on the proceeds from their farm. Life went well for a while till things went down south and a famine broke out. The farms and the crops planted began to gradually dry out. When everyone in the community was on the verge of giving up, Williams found a text book in a library he had been visiting (he dropped out of school and thought to make up for it by reading in the library). The book was called *Using Energy*- this was the book that would forever change his life and his community too. In the book, he saw a picture of a windmill and in that moment, caught the vision to build one in his small community to power the irrigation facilities and also generate electricity. Despite being called mad or high on hard drugs by even his own family, Williams built the wind vane from scraps of bicycles, cars, tyres etc. He built a wind mill that powered his house – the lights, radio, and soon enough the community began to charge their gadgets in his house. As time progressed, he went on to build a second one. This was a teenager who had dropped out of school due to the economic hardship his family faced; he had no formal learning in Physics or electronics. He took initiative and placed a high demand on his intelligence fuelled by the mindset of possibility that he had after reading that book.

You also can take initiative. When you place a demand on your intelligence, you immediately become resourceful. The kind of technology and connectivity we have in the world today has given us an unrestricted platform to be creative. Intelligence births creativity.

In the journey to success, you must be willing to ask a lot of questions. Intelligent people have more questions than they have answers. They have a holy curiosity and seem to question everything in a bid to reduce the level of ignorance they have about how things work. Einstein particularly said, "I have no special talent. I am only passionately curious." At another time he said, *"Imagination is more important than knowledge."* This was proof that he valued his ability to pry into the unknown than for him to rest upon the oars of things he had discovered before. Intelligence comes with the awareness that what you know is not enough for where you want to go. Put differently, what you know is not enough for where you dream to be. Einstein articulates this better and said, "*As a human being, one has been endowed with just enough intelligence to be able to see clearly how inadequate that intelligence is when confronted with what exists.*"

So, perhaps you are a genius in the making. You need to tap into your creativity, place a demand on your intelligence and take initiative.

> *In the journey to success, you must be willing to ask a lot of questions.*

Develop a personal Regimen: In the words of John Dryden, *"we first make our habits, and then our habits make us."* In the early years of Elon Musk (now Billionaire founder of SpaceX, CEO of TESLA and others), he read so much that he ran out of books to read in the library. He then went on to read the entire Encyclopaedia Britannica. Much later, he would read for 10 hours a day. He was a voracious reader. Bill Gates, when he started Microsoft, worked 16 hours a day for 5 years. For these five years, he inspected every line of code written by his company to ensure that quality was delivered. Thomas Edison was constantly at work and created several patented inventions. These men developed this as a habit. What is your own habit? What will it take for you to become the success that you dream of? Those who are at the top of the ladder today climbed there. They never wished themselves into that height of relevance. You would have to develop a set of habits to match the colourful future that you envisage for yourself. Don't expect to become a billionaire without giving a billion-dollar effort. It takes more than having a dream to achieve success. You have to become the dream. This is possible by adopting a new set of habits and dropping ones that will lead you away from the direction of your dreams.

Embrace failure early in your journey: World renowned leadership expert, John C. Maxwell wrote a book titled Failing Forward. Sounds like a weird title when we compare what failure does to most people that we know. The greatest threat to our success in life is failure, or in better words, the fear of failure. At certain points in our lives, we may have experienced failure, or someone close to us must have experienced a setback. Perhaps your parents tried a business and they failed, or you had a relationship with someone you loved but failed. Unconsciously all these become reference points for us when trying to take steps on our dreams. Or you've heard so many statistics that those who do not achieve certain things at a particular age will not be able to achieve anything anymore; (Like if you are not rich at 40, forget it). Whatever reference point you have about failure informs your own fear not to take a chance on your own dreams. I recently read a piece in the classic book, outwitting the devil, written by Napoleon Hill. He said,

During my quarter-century of research into the causes of success and failure, I have discovered principles of truth which have been helpful to me and to others. But nothing I have observed has impressed me more than the discovery that every great leader of the past, whose record I have examined, was beset by difficulties and met with temporary defeat before "arriving."

When you dive in, prepare for failure. The most powerful fear you must conquer is the fear of getting started. Here's what Napoleon Hill has to say about fear;

"FEAR is the tool of a man-made devil.

Self-confident faith in one's self is both the man-made weapon which defeats this devil and the man-made tool which builds a triumphant life. And it is more than that.

It is a link to the irresistible forces of the universe which stand behind a man who does not believe in failure and defeat as being anything but temporary experiences."

> *The most powerful fear you must conquer is the fear of getting started.*

There is a way life begins to bring things into alignment when you dare to take action on your dreams and to bring to fruition the ideas that dance in your imagination. So, develop a thick skin for failure. You should begin to say to yourself from the first thought "I won't rest until what I see on the inside becomes the reality that exists for me on the outside."

I'd like to end this chapter with the metaphor I learned about the stonecutter.

Your boulder will split if you tenaciously hit at it

Motivational speakers use the metaphor of the stone cutter to create an analogy in the minds of people on the need to start and keep persisting on that same journey.

When a stone cutter has a big boulder (stone) before him, he begins to hit on it; sometimes hitting at one or different spots repeatedly. He may go at it for 100, 200 or 300 times without a sign that the stone will split. Passers-by may feel he's wasting his energy or that the stone is too hard. But, the stone cutter knows what he is doing. While others may hate the noise, and others despise his labour, the cutter knows his aim and refuses to be distracted by what he sees in front of him or what is happening around him. He keeps hitting, and probably at the 1000th hit, we hear rushing sounds. The huge stone gives way to that one hit.

Here's the point

It may seem to people who see this epic event that it was that final hit that made the stone break. But is it? Not at all. All the efforts in the right direction made by the stone-cutter combined to make the stone split at the time it did. The bottom-line here is that no effort you put in the direction of your dreams is a waste. Treasure every moment, value the process and enjoy the journey.

At the end of our lives, we would not be sad because of the things we failed at, we will be sad because of the things we never attempted to do. Make an attempt. Even though you do not win at first, like John Maxwell said, you will learn.

I say to you, your dream is achievable and within reach.

So,

Dive in.

Questions

1. What are the things holding you back from diving into the execution of that dream? Can you list out all the possible roadblocks?

2. Look intently at your list and begin to creatively write 3-5 solutions to them.

3. Write out one step you must begin to take each day towards the execution of that dream. Remember to do it despite the fear or inner distrust you may have of yourself.

CHAPTER THREE

Employ Yourself

No one ever achieved success who doubted his ability to do so.

Oluwatobi Adesanya

Recently in Nigeria, digital media channels exposed the level of mental decadence we suffer as a nation. This spurred me to start live videos on Facebook where I addressed this issue and proffered solutions to them. While these videos may be hilarious, it reveals something deeper and that is the fact that ignorance prevails within the very fabric of every society. One of the common trends is to find people who believe that success can only be achieved through the help of some external force or some measure of luck. The place of hard work, tenacity and perseverance has been shelved aside.

Though knowledge has increased at an alarming rate, the level of assimilation and application of the knowledge has been rather low. Most people remain poor, ill, or on average levels, because they have abdicated the responsibility for their success in life to others or imaginary helpers, who would show up one day, wave the magic wand (like the fairy godmother) and immediately put them on top of the world.

Now, I don't mean to say people are not important in the fulfilment of our dreams. That wouldn't be true because we all need people to achieve our dreams. The point here is that every form of achievement begins first, in the words of Napoleon Hill, from desire. I would add belief, courage, confidence and faith to that list. Where do all these originate from? It starts from within.

This means that the most important assets we need in our lives are within us.

A friend of mine once shared this on his Facebook wall and I found a lot of wisdom to take home from it:

We've always been told that we are "sitting on gold mines." Usually, this means we are surrounded by several opportunities waiting for us to tap them, or to refine them, if you may.

This is very true.

But, there is something more.

I found a quote in a book I once read that said, "More gold has been mined from the thoughts of men than has been taken from the earth." The quote was by Napoleon Hill

This reveals to me that I'm not only sitting on a gold mine but that I have a gold mine within me.

So what is the conclusion of the matter?

If you cannot find the mine (with its gold) within you, you may never be able to find the mine (with its gold) which is around you.

You are not only sitting on a gold mine; you have a gold mine within you.

The biggest lesson I can pick from this is that **I have the gold mine within me.** More gold exists within me than there will be in the world. So, the concern for you should be starting with the man in the mirror.

Before I proceed, I invite you to make these confessions out loud to yourself:

All the dreams I seek to achieve are within me

I have what it takes to birth them

I will not delegate the responsibility for the fulfilment of my potentials and dreams to anyone

I have something to offer and I know that

It is enough.

Now we can proceed.

One of the biggest reasons fielded by youths for not living their dream is the lack of capital (this is particularly true for those who have the desire to run their own businesses). This reason has almost become a cliché proudly and loftily spoken of. Though we cannot underestimate the importance of financial capital when starting a business, money still should be the stumbling block. The moment an idea lands in your consciousness and you begin to express it in your conversation, the business has started already. Take for example a woman who is pregnant. The very first week she conceives she may not know until months have passed. This is how it happens with ideas too. You may not have set up the systems and structures for your business as yet, but since you already started to think and brainstorm on the plans and steps to achieve it, the business has kicked off.

When people think of running their own businesses, they think of a plush office with a serene environment, a mahogany desk and a secretary waiting outside the door to do their every bidding. Businesses don't start at the top- they start at the very bottom. We talked about self-made billionaires in the very first chapter. They practically MADE THEMSELVES into what they are today. They did not start by having a plush office and some fancy title. Rather they got their hands dirty all in the effort to make their dreams become a reality. So, **you need to be the first employee of your business**. You need to resume work as any other person would, or you would if you worked for someone else. Create a regimen around that idea. Do one thing every day, or apply the rule of 5 by John Maxwell on your idea every day as it comes to you. You have the responsibility to birth your dream and to manifest your potential. You cannot delegate that to anyone to do on your behalf.

This chapter is written to help you understand the place of PERSONAL RESPONSIBILITY. No one is going to do for you what you should do for yourself. You are enough to match your task. As a matter of fact, people only follow those who are on a destination and not those who give lip service to their ideas.

Billionaires always think ABUNDANCE and not SCARCITY. The word scarcity in itself is a relative word. Scarcity means a shortage in availability of a particular resource. For instance, we were taught in Economics about money and one of the things they taught us was that money is scarce. Is it? Scarcity is defined as the state of being short or in limited supply. I've often thought that if something is scarce it means that it is available in some places and barely available in other places.

> Billionaires always think
> ABUNDANCE and not SCARCITY.

Things do not just happen; there are principles behind whatever results we see in the world. Money and wealth only flow to areas where the value is being created. Where there is production and creation of value, money and

94

financial instruments flow there. Today, banks chase down successful business owners to give them loans, even when they have no need of it. The banks understand that they have the capacity to pay back their money with interest. The billionaires know what to do with the money that will yield results in multiple folds. So, one mindset you must drop is SCARCITY. You have to adopt the PROSPERITY MINDSET. A mindset that says, I have everything I need in abundance.

Those things that you need are first on your inside before they are found on the outside.

> *No one is going to do for you what you should do for yourself.*

If you cannot employ yourself in the fulfilment of your dreams, then do not expect others to be willing to work on them for you.

Please take a moment and say again to yourself

I came loaded with the potential to achieve all of my dreams. I am not limited by anything. I have all I need to fulfil my purpose.

Certain mindsets that limit people from seeing what they truly own. When you buy a new product from the marketplace, for example, an iPhone, it comes with everything in its pack. It comes loaded to function. As a matter of fact, some other products you buy come with a seal that tells you not to buy if the seal is broken. This shows that the manufacturer is certain that the best use of the product is tied to its completion when delivered to the customer. In other words, we can say for every one of us that each of us is born COMPLETE. We came to earth fully loaded – nothing missing.

80% of the success or failure we experience in life is tied to the use of our mind. The mind is a terrible thing to waste. The mindsets we have set the tone for the quality of life that we live. I'd be addressing common mindsets that hold people down from employing themselves.

Common reasons why people fail to employ themselves

If there is ever a thing so cheaply produced and sold without a price, it is the six-letter word – EXCUSE. There is an excuse for almost anything in the world. Here are some reasons, or put differently, excuses why people fail to employ themselves:

❖ **Focusing on weaknesses:** a fraction of every population suffer from one disability or the other. In Nigeria, where I come from, disabled people litter the streets with their families begging for alms from passers-by. Others may not be on the streets; they may be within good communities, but a personal weakness which may be physical, mental or some other disability prevents them from making the decision to work on their dreams. While there are countless people who are disabled and beggarly, there are a few who have stood out of the pack - who despite their disability chose to find ability in their weakness and turn it to a source of strength for their dreams.

Sometime in March 2017, I was privileged to meet Cobhams Asuquo. He is a blind musicologist, song producer, proud husband and father. At one time, he spoke about the gift of blindness and how this has helped him achieve success in life (more on this later). To many who have sight, calling "blindness" a "gift" seems out of place. But the result speaks. He has achieved more success than several other "seeing" people have. He chose to find ability in his disability. He chose to trust himself to achieve that which he saw in his imagination. He may not have been born with sight, but he had vision. He could see, even in his blindness, a future of possibilities where he would be able to produce quality music that the world will be inspired by. Then we have Stevie

Wonder, and the remarkable man, Nick Vijucic- the man who lives his life without limbs. These people employed themselves. They did not give an excuse that they could not work on their dream. They were their first capital and not money.

Consider this:

If you desire to start a business, you must realise that you are your own first capital. If you require a capital of 1 million to start, calculate how much your time and effort is worth, then subtract that from whatever you were looking for at first. When you are done, you can at least start with your sweat capital before seeking for further money from others.

> *If you desire to start a business,*
> *you must realise that you are your*
> *own first capital.*

Life without Limbs

The average human is born complete and functional from birth. But that was not the case with Nick Vijucic. Nick was born over 30 years ago with a rare condition where he came without arms and legs. He was every bit a normal child, only that he had no arms or legs. His parents refused to treat him any different from his other siblings; they enrolled him in a school like every normal kid. In no time, he became a centre of attraction for bullies who picked on him at every given opportunity. He lost his self-esteem and soon was spiralling down the path of depression. He even thought to drown himself in the bathtub at one time.

Remembering the love his parents had for him, he chose not to take his own life and that began his path to finding purpose. Today, he travels the world speaking to millions of people annually. He has met Presidents of nations and now runs an NGO aside his other businesses. To his name are several best-selling books which have continued to inspire the world. The amazing thing is that he lives a normal life with his family and does everything anyone could ever do. He is a lovely father and husband in his family, works from his office, swims and plays golf. He chose to look beyond his perceived limitation and found a way to live his dreams. As he does so, he is inspiring millions of other people in the world to live their dreams as well. You **only have limits when you set one for yourself** (Please read that again). Nick has set no limits for himself on what he could do; he keeps on going and living his dreams. Something tells me that you reading this have arms and legs and at least you are fully functional. So, what is limiting you? What physical impairment do you have that limits you from where you dream of?

Though you may feel you cannot achieve what you dream of, you must proceed as if those limitations do not exist. One quote I read says, "If you've got the mind to dream it up and the capacity to believe in accomplishing that dream, let nothing or no one get in the way of it." That's the truth.

There's a champion, a global success in every child is born into the world, no matter the limitation that the child may come with.

The Gift of Blindness

That's what Cobhams says. The blind are gifted, even if they lack sight. He found vision and that has taken him places those who have sight only dream of. His story reminds me of the famous quote by Helen Keller (who from 18 months lost her sense of hearing, sight and speech), she said, "The only thing worse than being blind is having sight but no vision." Myles Munroe also said repeatedly that, "The greatest gift God gave to man is not sight but vision." So, what's your excuse?

What you need to EMPLOY YOURSELF

You need LOVE: you have to love yourself first. There are certain things about your life that cannot change and there are others that can. Michael Jackson sang the song, "I'm starting with the man in the mirror." That's the way it works. You have to start by loving everything about you. You should have a healthy self-perception. How people see you begins first from how you perceive yourself. You must develop positive and empowering views about who you are. Think positive thoughts, thoughts of love, hope and possibility. When you start to love yourself, you will come to a place of personal power where you can begin to handle life and walk in the direction of your dreams. One quote that fits well into this says,

God grant me the serenity to accept the things I cannot change, the courage to change the things I can, and the wisdom to know the difference.

-Reinhold Niebuhr

Maya Angelou, the famous Poet, once said, *"If you don't like something, change it. If you can't change it, change your attitude."* There are many things within our power to alter. Things like our mindset, habits, relationships, skill level, amongst others. But there are other things like our height, race, gender, family background etc. which are fixed. These are things we must accept and live by.

Then you must love others genuinely. The way we treat others is a projection of how we treat ourselves. The way we love others is a projection of how much we love ourselves. The Holy Bible tells us to love our neighbours as ourselves. When you have genuine love for others, you begin to have ideas on how to help, how to solve the problems of humanity and that's where impact begins. With love, comes acceptance. Those who don't live their dreams do not love themselves enough. Loving oneself enough involves finding ways you can bring happiness into the lives of those around you. No one loves to keep a liability. Why do people love celebrities? It isn't only because of the good looks or money-in-the-bank. It is because of the contributions they make to the lives of others. A simple look at the profiles of celebrities in Hollywood, music artiste, authors etc., will reveal that they add value to others in some way. So you want to be loved? Then you need to answer this question- what value can I give to others? Because the true measure of love (for yourself and others) is in what you do and not feelings. Love is nothing if it is not demonstrated.

Take an inventory of what you have: Remember the gold mine illustration? Motivational speakers share endless stories of how people found an opportunity but lost it –more like "Three feet from gold." This could create anxiety. In a subtle way, these stories create a divide and raise a question in the minds of people. Questions like, *"So, how do I find my gold mine?"* *"Hope I haven't missed my gold mine?"* *"My friend found his, I doubt if I can ever find mine"* Believe it or not, these thoughts and more go on in the minds of people. But, the reality is; you are not only surrounded by a gold mine, you have a gold mine within you. You are a walking Gold Mine.

So, take inventory of what you have. You have a gold mine within you waiting to be tapped; you are a walking billionaire. There's one verse I found in the Bible that describes the ideas I expressed. Those who work their land will have abundant food, but those who chase fantasies will have their fill of poverty

This reveals to me that we all have a land, or put differently, a gold mine which we are supposed to tap and mine from; you have potentials within you. I'm convinced that the wealthiest spot on earth is not the physical gold mines in South Africa or the Oil wells in the Middle East or the large population of China. The wealthiest spot on earth is your mind – that gold mine that you carry on your inside.

Make this confession

I am a walking gold mine.

I have what it takes to succeed at whatever I do

The wisdom and intelligence I need to mine my gold is within reach

I rest at nothing till my "gold" is refined and I become what I dream of

NB: Your gold here would best be described as your ideas, your talents and potentials.

> *You have to rise up and take action and own the process that leads to the fulfilment of your vision.*

You need to take Personal Responsibility: Some of the most important things we do on a daily basis cannot be delegated. If such things are delegated, it must be as a result of some sort of ailment. Feeding, using the restroom, breathing and thinking amongst other things are what we do on a daily basis to guarantee our survival. What if you chose not to eat because no one was there to feed you, you may end up starving to death. I'm trying to make you realise that responsibility for oneself must go beyond survival to significance. In the event of a fire outbreak, everyone runs towards the direction of safety irrespective of others that may be with them. Without thinking, each person takes responsibility for him/herself. In the same way, we must see living a life of success in every aspect of life as that. You must have a mindset that says **"It is up to me to make things happen"** **"It is up to me to live out my dreams."** You have to rise up and take action and own the process that leads to the fulfilment of your vision. You may delegate anything in life, but you cannot delegate the bringing to pass of your vision. You have to be fully involved. There is a reason why that idea came to you. There is a bigger reason behind why that vision was conceived by you at this time. It reveals that you have the ability to make it happen and that several others will benefit from it.

The J.K Rowling Example and why you need to Employ Yourself

There are only a few authors who have recorded such remarkable feats as Rowling. Her story is a typical representation of a grass-to-grace scenario.

Seven years after she completed her university education, her life appeared to have come to a halt. She was a wreck. She could well fit the description of a failure. During this period, her marriage failed, she lost her job and still had a daughter to care for with no one to assist her. At a time, she was diagnosed with clinical depression and attempted to commit suicide. Much later, with a typewriter, she began writing her books. It was said that her emotional, financial and physical travails informed the characters she used in the Harry Potter series. In 2004, she became the first writer to be named a US Dollar billionaire by writing books. The sale of the Harry Potter series on the first day of release was up to 11 million copies. She is a phenomenal success and a perfect example of one who **employed herself.** She used her adversity to gain momentum. Her choice to **employ** her writing gift opened unimaginable doors for her.

When you take inventory of your gifts and talents, matched with courage, confidence and diligence, you can turn any adverse situation around you into something remarkable. You have what it takes to transform your current life into that which you dream of.

Questions

1. Take the different confessions in this chapter for 7 days and make them a part of your daily routine. It will begin to change your perspective about who you are.

2. How can you begin to perceive your limitations differently?

3. There is an ability in every disability. How can you begin to use that which limited you before as a tool for inspiring others and living a better life?

CHAPTER FOUR

Ignore Detractors

"Keep away from people who belittle your ambitions. Small people always do that, but the really great make you feel that you, too, can become great."

--Mark Twain

Accept it. If you are going to be successful, you must be ready to have haters around you. A detractor will be best described by the popular slang *haters*. I found a perfect definition for who *haters* are. **Haters are people who think they know the route to success but they never actually get on the plane to fly there.** For a more technical definition, a detractor is someone who puts you down. When you are proposing ideas. A detractor is a person who finds fault with everything you say. Have you met such people? Whether you have or not, everyone knows the experience is not always pleasant.

> *I found a perfect definition for who haters are. Haters are people who think they know the route to success but they never actually get on the plane to fly there.*

Lessons from Football:

Sports, especially the game of football unites the world in such an amazing way. Besides the excitement, there are lessons which can be applied to other areas of life as well.

How does it feel to walk into a stadium aware that up to 50% of the audience is against you and your team and want you to lose the game? Not good, right? Teams still go on to play and win despite the huge statistic against them. So, what do these players (11 of them) do? They focus on the game, play to win and celebrate those who are for them, while ignoring boos from the fans of their opponent.

You may not be a football player or into sports, but as long as you wake up each day and get off your bed; you step into the game of life. Life is more like a football game. Some will stand with you through the thick-and-thin, while others stand at a distance to throw stones at your 'glass house'. I may not be able to explain why people choose to be haters, but one thing I know is, listening to detractors will never get you to the place you dream of.

If there is one thing to note about life, it is that not everyone is headed in the same direction you are. It is best to identify those who are going your direction and excuse those who aren't. Just as a football player on the pitch will not intentionally pass the ball to an opponent, even so, you must be intentional with those you choose to hang around with.

> *If there is one thing to note about life, it is that not everyone is headed in the same direction you are.*

Lessons from our conscious mind

One peculiar characteristic of billionaires is that they pursue few things, but fiercely. They are committed to their goals, and that's why they make it simple and short. Steve Jobs calls this KISS; which means *Keep It Simple and Stupid.* They have no tolerance for whatever hinders them from achieving their aim.

If we took out time to study how the mind works, some amazing revelations may invade your mind. I found out that the conscious mind can only hold about 7-9 thoughts per time. The brain finds a unique way to shut out whatever is not relevant to whatever we are working on at that time. This means that while we may be surrounded by naysayers and haters, we can choose those to allow into our thinking space. Since we can only focus on a handful of things at a time.

How do you handle detractors?

A YouTube video garnered a lot of views during Obama's tenure as President of the United States of America. No, it wasn't when he gave those riveting speeches that commanded a standing ovation or caused a tear. Rather, it was one where a young boy asked him a simple question. He said, *"Why do people hate you?"* This question opened up the door of knowledge to the young kid. Obama gave an apt response.

Here are some of the things he mentioned; *"I did get elected as President of America, so that means not everyone hates me. Many of the things you see are simply people playing politics to* **promote their own interest** *–more like people trying to poke you….* **as long as you are going in the right direction, you only have to ignore the distractions.** *I'm a pretty tough guy…."* **Paraphrase and emphasis mine**

This response captures the essence of this chapter. So, let's see how Billionaires get this done:

✚ **A clear sense of purpose and direction:** Having clarity on your destination reduces hassles and creates an opportunity for proper planning. One characteristic of self-made billionaires is the simplicity of purpose. Henry Ford wanted to democratise the mobile. Bill Gates wanted to a PC in every home in the world; Elon Musk wants to bring civilisation to Mars. Great achievers are point clear on what they want and what they cannot settle for. They are addicted to seeing results in whatever they get involved in. A clear sense of purpose provides direction for decisions and projects embarked on.

> *Having clarity on your destination reduces hassles and creates an opportunity for proper planning.*

+ **They identify the detractors:** Sometimes we may have to let go of our best associates, or our best associate may leave for another dream they consider more realistic. Mark Zuckerberg, Founder of Facebook, at a point in the life of the company had this challenge. While speaking at the graduation of the class of 2017 at Harvard University where he received his degree; see his words;

A couple years in, some big companies wanted to buy us. I didn't want to sell. I wanted to see if we could connect more people. We were building the first News Feed, and I thought if we could just launch this, it could change how we learn about the world.

Nearly everyone else wanted to sell. Without a sense of higher purpose, this was the StartUp dream come true. It tore our company apart. After one tense argument, an advisor told me if I didn't agree to sell, I would regret the decision for the rest of my life. Relationships were so frayed that within a year or so every single person on the management team was gone. That was my hardest time leading Facebook. I *believed in what we were doing, but I felt alone. And worse, it was my fault. I wondered if I was just wrong, an imposter, a 22-year-old kid who had no idea how the world worked. Now, years later, I understand that *is* how things work with no sense of higher purpose. It's up to us to create it so we can all keep moving forward together.*

Excerpts of Speech Delivered at Harvard University Class of 2017

By Mark Zuckerberg

It is clear that Mark had a dream, a big one –to impact the world. One thing that you can't afford to ignore is the reality that not everyone sees what you see. From the moment you are clear about where you are headed, either to create a global business or to start a social enterprise, not everyone who started with you will always be there as the years go by.

Sometimes you have to let go of the good to reach forth to the great things that lay ahead. No one knows how things will turn out in the end. We can only predict, but the one who stays put to his dream has an increased chance of achieving his dream.

> *Sometimes you have to let go of the good to reach forth to the great things that lay ahead.*

Why you should not listen so much to experts

Almost in every field of endeavour, there are experts who we go-to for advice and to predict the business. Connecting the dots from history, you'd see there has always been lines of impossibility which they believed could never be crossed. Every generation seems to have its own definition of what it terms impossible, only to be proved wrong by the next generation. In other words, we keep expanding the limits of what we call "impossible." Nelson Mandela is often quoted as saying, *"It is not impossible, it only hasn't been done yet."*

Why is this important?

Most of the impossibilities in each generation can be traced to the experts of their time. While knowledge can be liberating, it can also be limiting. When the future is predicted based on the things that have occurred before or that are in existence, we put a limit on what is possible in the future. Einstein foresaw this when he said, *"Imagination is more important than knowledge."* Your detractors may not be the friend next door, or the reporter in the tabloids trying to talk down your great initiative. It may be that professional you go to for consultation or advice on how to birth your dream. Much worse it could be a member of your board –like Zuckerberg, who advise to 'sell your company' instead of showing support.

The next time you are on a flight to any choice destination, remember that in 1902, a physicist and Director of the US Naval Observatory, Simon Newcomb said, with resounding firmness and certainty that, "Flight by machines heavier than air is impractical and insignificant, if not utterly impossible." Barely a year later, Wilbur and Oliver Wright, working at their little bicycle workshop shattered this expert hypothesis and birthed the aviation industry. Today, man has not only defied the law of gravity in travelling from one location to another on earth, we have broken into outer space to land man on the moon. Never underestimate the conclusions of the "experts" –it may limit you if believed. When you take a shot at your dreams, you'd realise that impossibility is only a word and not reality.

> *When the future is predicted based on the things that have occurred before or that are in existence, we put a limit on what is possible in the future.*

If you dream of the achievement of a thing, then it proves two things- that it is possible, and you have the ability to achieve it.

What we can learn from Elon Musk

While the world is in awe of great companies like Google, Facebook, Amazon and others, there is one man leading revolution not only in the business space but in the technology space as well. His companies and what they stand for have global relevance. I'm talking about the founder of PayPal, Tesla, Space X and more recently, The Boring Company –a rather sarcastic name for a company. This man is defying odds against the trends to build Tesla which in decades from now could see the end of gasoline powered vehicles in the world if other manufacturers do not embrace innovation. The level of an affront against his growing venture can be felt, but he remains relentless. He is not only committed to creating automobiles that would contribute to a safer climate, he wants to take man to Mars. He once said, "I want to die on Mars, only not on impact." When you seek for a model that is undeterred by naysayers, think of Elon. Being a billionaire, even been a success at anything, requires laser-like focus and full commitment. Pursuing your dream is not a 9-5 routine, it is a lifelong process.

In wrapping this up, I'd say when people try to put you down, realise that they are already down. You should identify early enough, those who will make it easier to achieve your dreams and those who will take you far away from it. Not everyone is on the same journey as you are. You will do yourself a lot of good by believing early enough that you are responsible for your success or wealth in life.

<u>Questions</u>

1. Take an inventory of those in your life, list them from 1-20. Ensure that the list contains the names of some of the most important people in your life. The task here is to come up with just 10 indispensable people (those you cannot just do without). Now, start eliminating them from the bottom and come up with a list of 10 people.

2. Repeat this exercise for every area of your life –family, business, workplace association and every other group you may belong to.

The benefit of this exercise is that it finally helps you to see those who are contributing the most to your life and those who are contributing the least to your growth and towards the achievement of your dreams in life. What did you find out? Who will you be spending more time with now?

See you in the next chapter...

CHAPTER FIVE

Commitment to constant improvement

The only true security in life comes from knowing that every single day you are improving yourself.

-Tony Robbins

*I*magine you dashed out from your five-star apartment driving out your Lamborghini Murciélago and while racing at 200km/h you found out the fuel tank is on empty and your jolly ride is brought to an abrupt stop. What do you do? Thankfully, you sight a filling station just a few blocks away and you trick the car to get it filled and voila! You are on your jolly ride to your destination. Hopefully, you arrive in time.

This is the logical thing to do: fuel your car and move on. But, James who lives just down your street doesn't think so. He works three jobs and drives a 2003 Volkswagen car that he fixes every other day. He cradles along the road as the car lets out sounds that cause school children around to laugh. One time, his car breaks down on the road while heading to his second job. Though he sighted a fuel station afar, he alighted from his car –almost tripping off, and started to push the car to his destination. For James, the destination was more important than the means to get there. He exerts the last ounce of strength he had. Thinking it wise, he chose to save his money and exert all the energy in the process. He got to the meeting 90 minutes. And if your guess is as good as mine, he was completely unproductive.

What do you think of James?

…………………………………

Hopefully, you are not James. If your guess is as good as mine, you want to be the guy/lady who drives out in a Lamborghini Murcielago or Lamborghini Miura to wherever you're going. While the illustration may be far from reality (or perhaps not) this reveals the way most people live their lives. The race to become something, to be more successful, to earn a higher income and for some, to keep up with the Joneses; keeps a lot of people in a lifestyle that limits them for life.

I learnt about the "Rat-race" when I read the evergreen-best-selling book from Robert Kiyosaki, *Rich Dad Poor Dad.* He revealed how his poor dad worked his life out earning an income, acquiring liabilities and ended up broke just like everyone else. Why was this so? Why was he different from the *Rich Dad?* The difference was in what they invested in.

The rich invest in improvement –which comes in various forms- Personal, mental, social, knowledge, financial, spiritual; while the poor stay on the pursuit of materials and experiences to feel comfortable.

Billionaires are aware of the need for constant replenishment and so they go after knowledge, exposure, training and everything they need to stay renewed.

The very nature of life begs for evolution and constant improvement. In Charles Darwin theory of Natural Selection, he essentially states that only the "strong" survive. Since change is constant in every age, only the organisms that are best suited to the prevailing conditions will be able to compete and survive. In other words, the ability to adapt consistently through changing times results in survival and continual existence. There are hundreds of species that have gone into extinction and several others today are at the brink of this. What does this tell us? It reveals to us that there is a need to constantly evolve. Even though we may not change from being human to Elephant, we must improve the quality of our lives to capture and seize new opportunities. Remember the opening quote, *"The only true security in life comes from knowing that every single day you are improving yourself."*

So, are you improving?

This chapter will provide answers to the areas you should be constantly evolving on a daily basis.

We may not be able to change our lives overnight, but we can change our decisions overnight and over time our lives will change for the better.

> *Billionaires are aware of the need for constant replenishment and so they go after knowledge, exposure, training and everything they need to stay renewed.*

Jolted to reality

A time came in the life of a man in his 30's who had lived a mediocre life working as a Janitor in a small company. He lived in the basement of a house and drove an old car which was a pain-in-the-heart. One night, he woke up and chose not to settle for anything less in life anymore. This single decision in a room where no one else was radically changed his life. 10 years down the line, he was flying over a city to one of the seminars he had put together and realised there was an enormous traffic jam on the way to the centre. Seeing the traffic jam, he thought to himself that whatever was going in that city was sure going to affect the attendance of people at his seminar. Only moments after he arrived did he realise that the traffic jam and the crowd he saw were people coming over to his seminar.

This man is Tony Robbins. He runs 31 companies today, is a best-selling author and has affected the lives of millions of people in several continents of the world.

He chose not to settle for less but chose to set higher standards which he will not fall short of for anything. If there is any standard you should set for yourself, it is to give yourself to constant improvement. Abraham Lincoln who is considered one of the greatest American

Presidents once said, *"I have little respect for a man who is not more wiser today than he was yesterday."* He was referring to the same thing – improvement.

The goose and golden egg

The story is told of a farmer who had a goose. One fateful day he came into his barn and went to his goose only to realise that she had laid golden eggs. The farmer took it up, examined the egg to know if what he saw was really good fortune smiling on him. He ran out of his barn, showed his wife and they sold it. The next day, he came again and found eggs of gold in the nest of the goose- they couldn't explain how this came about. It was only days afterwards and their fortune began to change. They became rich overnight. After a while, the farmer grew greedy –his curiosity had a huge part to play in this too-as they say, curiosity killed the cat but in this case curiosity (let me add greed) killed the goose. Days later, the farmer could not wait for another day to get his eggs; he took a knife and killed the goose. To his utter surprise, there was no egg in the goose –not even its shell had been developing on the inside of it. You know what happened next- their lucky dip dried up and with it the goose. There were no more golden eggs and of course, no more goose.

Don't we also make this same mistake too? We do not take care of our "goose." In this case, the goose is you. You do not take time out to replenish yourself. You fail to take a break from the course of life to find renewed strength, vision, direction and hope for the future. While you may be in the pursuit of some financial goal, spiritual goal or some relationship goal, do not forget that you are your most important asset.

Do not keep on chasing things at the expense of your own development. The quality of results you can produce at any given time is directly related to how well you are at any given time.

> *You need a fertile mind that conceives wholesome, deep thoughts and ideas that are capable of transforming a place and the people around you.*

Successful people give themselves to exercise, healthy diets, relaxation. They also feed their minds with the right materials that enhance the level of their thinking. If you want to be very successful, you cannot afford to have a stale mind. You need a fertile mind that conceives wholesome, deep thoughts and ideas that are capable of transforming a place and the people around you. Don't keep on doing the same thing you've been doing and expect a different result –someone referred to that as madness.

Embrace constant and never ending improvement. Begin to develop a desperate hunger and desire to be better the next time. A story has it that a real estate developer and builder was once asked, *"Which of these building projects do you consider your most beautiful and successful venture?"* To the utmost surprise of the interviewer, he said, "The next one." Be better, do things better, keep on improving on your last performance. Don't be so impressed by your last performance that you forget to improve on it.

Countries that focus more on their human capital development tend to produce a wealthier populace. This is often reflected in the kind of education received by its institutions and the freedom given to people to explore and fulfil potential. The reason why first world nations are prosperous is that they have chosen to tap into the immense treasure in human potential. Beyond personal and individual development, institutions can be set up to develop great minds who can bring prosperity to any place.

Keys to constant improvement

Tai Lopez identifies five things one can do to have a good life, but I see that differently –in many ways, they are vital keys to improvement.

Find mentors to help you grow:

Mentors aren't just teachers who reveal a bunch of principles or "steps" to live by. A mentor is an awakener that quickens his mentee to rise up to the greatness that dwells within. Recently, I experienced a dramatic transformation in my social life because my mentor is very emotional. This has helped me develop empathy and get an instant connection to people irrespective of who they are. Irrespective of whatever success you have recorded, there are always others who have ten times the results you have. There is no gap or neutral ground in nature. It is either you are dying or you're living. When you find people who are doing way better than you, you'd find the needed inspiration to keep on succeeding and being your best. One of the biggest lies you can believe is that you are finished.

How would you feel if the founder of Walmart, Sam Walton, Jeff Bezos of Amazon decides to partner with you in your business? Your chances of succeeding in that line of business will be almost 99%. Why? You have some of the brightest minds and most successful people to help you grow through the tough times. With their knowledge, experience and personal results, you are certain that you would go through the toughest times and attain success.

> *Some of the most successful people in the world were mentored by someone who also served as mentors to others.*

Some of the most successful people in the world were mentored by someone who also served as mentors to others. Bill Gates has enjoyed the mentorship of Warren Buffet for several years running. They had their first contact when Bill's mum put together a dinner where Warren was also invited. This chance meeting sparked up a discussion about business and philanthropy. They connected on these subject matters though their areas of business were different. Mark Zuckerberg; Founder Facebook had the chance to be mentored by Steve Jobs before he passed on. The famous Oprah Winfrey enjoyed the mentorship of Maya Angelou (the famous Poet). Virgin Group Co-founder; Richard Branson also had the support of Sir Freddie Laker who was a British airline entrepreneur. The list goes on. Mentors edge us on when we feel like giving up. They see potential in areas of our lives where we may be unaware. If you desire to improve, then you must spend more time with mentors than you spend with your friends. Keeping company with those on your level keeps you on that same level for a long time.

Jim Rohn once said, *"You are the average of the five people you spend the most time with."* From now on, you must make a commitment to spend more time with those who are already where you are going.

> *A mentor is an awakener that quickens his mentee to rise up to the greatness that dwells within.*

Evaluate yourself:

Socrates, the famous Greek philosopher, once said: *"The unexamined life is not worth living."* When I watch documentaries, especially of famous plane crashes in history, I'm amazed at the level of details people give to finding the cause of such accidents. In 1977, 40 years ago, an incident considered one of the greatest airplane mishaps in history occurred. Two Boeing 747 jets collided on the airport runway. It had been a well-planned take-off for both planes, but they had to be diverted due to threats at their agreed destinations. As they attempted to do another take-off from the airport, there was a miscommunication between the pilots of the planes and the watchtower. This, coupled with a fog that settled on the tarmac made it impossible for the pilots to see where they were headed. While one of the pilots missed his turn, the other pilot was steaming on to take off. It was only when the planes were too close for the impact that they realised they were head on to one another. The pilots tried to avoid the mishap by veering away, but the planes collided and in moments, both planes went up in flames with series of explosion. 583 people died in that mishap. As with all mishaps in history, they investigated the event and realised that a chain of factors caused the tragic event. One pilot didn't receive clear instructions to take-off and missed his runway coupled with the clouds. Looking at these factors, one would see that there were certain events which were within human control except the fog which was clearly out of human control. The reason why we can have this information is that the incident was investigated. Evaluation here speaks of making inquiry into how something went. You do not need to wait till you have experienced a setback before you take an evaluated look at your life.

Setbacks (which are always temporary) are a part of life; therefore, we can choose to always learn from them. John Maxwell wrote, *"Sometimes you win, and sometimes you learn."*

Ask yourself questions that make you see areas where you need improvement. Benjamin Franklin; one of the founding fathers of the United States, had a daily routine of questions he put up for himself. Every morning he asked, "What good will I do today?" Then in the evening, he asks himself, "What good have I done today?" Questions put us on our toes. If you're having a challenge now, ask, "What is good about this problem?" "How can I tackle this same challenge next time?" "What areas of my life do I need to change?" "How can I improve on my last performance?" When you begin to give yourself over to evaluation, you begin to turn your experience into wisdom. Evaluation helps you know that there is never an unprofitable experience.

> *Evaluation helps you know that there is never an unprofitable experience.*

Perseverance:

Nothing is ever built at once. Everything goes through a process and processes require not only time but great effort. Reality TV and other shows promoted by the media make it appear that achieving success could be instant. The truth is success comes at a cost and this cost cannot be delegated or wished away; there is a price for greatness. Perseverance is needed to reach the goal and to achieve the dream. No one is really a failure; failure only comes by not persevering enough. The moment you give up then comes your moment of failure. Failure shifts from being your reality when you choose to take on, again and again, the chance to live your dreams.

The Failure who became President

No other person can fit perfectly, the description of a failure more than Abraham Lincoln. But that is not what history later on records about him. He ended up being one of the best presidents America ever produced. He may not have been a billionaire, but he successfully steered a nation out of deep crisis and built a strong nation –a nation that today is home to over 500 billionaires. What made this man stand out? Above all qualities, it was his ability to persevere through the toughest of times. Abraham Lincoln failed several times from 1832-1858 before he became elected in 1860. He lost his job, failed in his business, lost his wife, had a nervous breakdown and was defeated in several elections where he vied for political office. He persevered through it all. What's the interesting part in this? Had he given up in 1858, he would have been forgotten and no one will ever remember that there once lived a man called Abraham Lincoln. Perhaps there were several other men and women like him who must have given up in the process and never became known. You can be that exception. Persevere through the thick and thin of birthing your idea and see your dreams come to pass. The pain of perseverance is far lesser (more rewarding) than the pain of regret. Keep on pushing.

> *Books are like portals or time machines, they transport us into the mind and experience of the writer.*

Books:

Books are like portals or time machines, they transport us into the mind and experience of the writer. With books, we can pick up skills, unlearn and learn new habits and become better at whatever we do. Though some of the top people in your field may be inaccessible to you, their books are always accessible. When you have your library filled with their books, you have the chance to imbibe the thoughts, mindsets and wisdom they have acquired. The price of a book is not really its price. When you look intently, you will realise you are only paying for the paper and its shipping and other logistic costs. Why do I say this? The experience, wisdom and lessons a writer shares are invaluable and they should be treasured by you –the reader. Tai Lopez says he reads a book a day, Mark Zuckerberg reads 4 books a month and the same goes for the successful. It is about time you stopped seeing reading as a hobby and start seeing it as a tool for personal improvement. Books are one of the quickest routes to self-development.

In concluding this chapter, I'd say *"The room for self-improvement is never filled. You just have to keep on getting better."*

Questions:

1. It's been said that *"It is madness to keep on doing the same thing and expecting a different result."* In the light of these, what have you been doing which you desire a change? Take an inventory of your life. Find out the things that are working and the things that are not.

2. Map out a strategy from what you learned in this chapter to continually improve on yourself.

3. Focus more on being productive and reduce your focus on products. This involves you investing more into yourself so you can produce better results. Take a course (online or in a formal school), learn a new skill, read a new book, go out of your way to learn about a part of the

world you never knew. Explore and never stop improving.

CHAPTER SIX

Think Globally

During bad a circumstance, which is the human inheritance, you must decide not to be reduced. You have your humanity, and you must not allow anything reduce that. We are obliged to know we are global citizens. Disasters remind us we are world citizens, whether we like it or not.

- Maya Angelou

rrespective of race, gender and nationality, we are all connected. Every child gets 50% of his DNA from their parent, and each parent also gets theirs from their parents too. In each generation, there is a transfer of genetic features from the previous to the present generation. When we look deeply into the fabric of our DNA's we realise that there is no need to be racist, nationalistic or bias about our colour or background.

In a study recently carried out, persons from different nationalities in the world took the DNA test. When the test result was out, it was revealed that each person had a percentage of all other races in their genome. You may be proud of your country –and we should be, but stereotypes have alienated us from ourselves. The greatest human achievement is yet to become a reality. It will only be so when we see ourselves as global citizens and not people divided by colour, location, race or religion. It is common to hear the media group countries as First world countries, underdeveloped, developing, third world nations. The media refers to third world nations as countries in Africa where poverty, unemployment, terrorism and other challenges are dominant. They refer to the first world nations as those who are developed or helpers to those who are less developed. We may not have the same status or levels of development, yet we have more things that unite us than those that divide us. Maya Angelou in the quote above mentions that it is only during adversity that we realise that we are not divided but that we are citizens of the world.

When you realise that you are connected in some way to others, the ideas and initiatives you involve in will go to a new level. Do not conceive dreams that can only affect you and those around you. It costs nothing to think BIGGER than you are doing right now. You must begin to think about how your actions can affect the lives of several people on earth today.

> *When you realise that you are connected in some way to others, the ideas and initiatives you involve in will go to a new level.*

The most successful people aren't only big dreamers but people that think globally. They think of how to affect the lives of billions of people on earth with their ideas, and initiatives. They expand their tents by being aware of the needs of people and taking steps to solve the problems. Sometimes ago, James Hansen said, "Climate change is not a prediction; it is happening right before our eyes". Musk and other influential personalities in diverse fields took the baton of responsibility to get things done as regards the change.

A research revealed that The United States of America has 62% of its billionaires who are self-made. This cannot be a coincidence. I believe it has to do with the ideals the country upholds. Looking at the Declaration of Independence, it states:

We hold these truths to be self-evident, that all men are created equal, that they are endowed by their Creator with certain unalienable Rights, that among these are Life, Liberty and the pursuit of Happiness.

> *The most successful people aren't only big dreamers but people that think globally.*

The United States has risen to become one of the top countries in the world that promote freedom and individualism. These ideals of freedom and liberty brought about the birth of capitalism. Capitalism is the ideology that formed the foundation of great corporations of the industrial age and raised several billionaires like Andrew Carnegie, Charles Schwab, Henry Ford amongst others. Today, that ideology has birthed even more billionaires than the industrial age. In 2016, Forbes stated that the Billionaires in the world were 1,810. Of this number, 584 of them are from the United States in America, while the others are shared amongst nations like China, Germany, India and Russia.

> *Begin to see yourself as a global citizen and not just a citizen of whatever country you are from.*

America has created an environment that allows for one to think globally. People of all races can be found in America and even foreigners who either migrated or settled there are flourishing. Michael Dell, Mark Zuckerberg and several others were originally not American by descent, but by migration and settlement, they have found a new place they could call home. On August 28, 1963, at Lincoln Memorial, Dr Martin Luther King Jr. gave a remarkable speech that has gone down in history as one of the greatest speeches ever given. He said. "I look to a day when people will not be judged by the colour of their skin, but by the content of their character." You will agree that the dream of Dr Martin Luther King Jr. still lives. It created in everyone a global mindset that was not painted by racism or any other form of discrimination.

So, whatever ideas you have about changing the world, multiply that by 7 billion people. Begin to see yourself as a global citizen and not just a citizen of whatever country you are from.

It is possible to raise too many billionaires in America because the nation has grown through the ranks and does not see itself as one that exists for its people alone. They have risen to become number one in the world and have maintained that for many years running. The American president is more or less the President of the world and receives that accolade; the level of responsibility attached to that office proves it. When you begin to adopt a global mindset, the possibility of succeeding and making greater impact multiplies.

So where do you start from?

Get away from stereotypes:

We learn about the world through stereotype. As we become accustomed to how the world works, we begin to classify things into groups which help to easily recognise things. While this is a normal learning process for every human being, stereotypes get out of hand when they are used derogatorily or led to prejudice others. Stereotypes have become more associated with negative views than positive views. If you want to be successful, then you've got to let go of any stereotype that paints people in a negative light. Joel Osteen, the Presiding Pastor over Lakewood Church once told the story of a woman who complains about her neighbour's dirty clothes. Whenever she looked out of her window, she would see their neighbour, a woman, constantly spread dirty clothes on the line. This went on repeatedly for days, until one day her husband decided to take a look at this daily occurrence that always got his wife talking. When he got to the window, he looked surprised. Not because he finally got to realise what his wife had been saying, but he saw that the window blinds of their house were dirty. Apparently, their uncleaned windows made the clean clothes appear dirty and stained. The way you see others says more about you than it does about them. This is because we judge people not based on how they really are, but on how we are.

> *If you want to be successful, then you've got to let go of any stereotype that paints people in a negative light.*

Put differently, the interpretation of the world is not as it is, but as we are. Since the way one sees the world informs our judgment, the information we have about others must be carefully screened before it is believed. Those who get the best out of a place or a person are those who have great belief in those places or persons. Ralph Waldo Emerson said, "Treat a man as he is, and he will remain as he is. Treat a man as he could be, and he will become what he should be." People tend to measure up to the standard that you place on them. To get the best out of life and from the people around you, you must invest a huge belief in them, affirming them of the potential they hold.

> *Believe the best of people. Avoid negative stereotypes or prejudging people.*

A research was carried out by psychologists where they tested subjects for this experiment. While examining their brain waves, they mentioned certain both positive and negative words. They then associated these words to names of White and Black people respectively. The result was their brain responded rapidly to these words proving affirmation and acceptance of this as normal. In most white countries where there are blacks, there is the tendency for blacks to be side-lined, murdered with impunity and treated less than their white counterparts. The media also promote this idea to the people – associating crime and violence to the black community while brilliance and patriotism is to the White people. This was the reason why the Black Lives Matter movement started up. You must choose to believe the best about people irrespective of what the media portrays. How in the world would people be able to build billion dollar businesses without people? Or should I say, without trusting people? Yes, there is the tendency for people to misbehave, but this does not deny the fact that there are several good people who will support a dream.

Believe the best of people. Avoid negative stereotypes or prejudging people.

See the world as your stage:

"All the world's a stage and all the men and women are merely players" so says, William Shakespeare. Your ideas are bound to go from

good to great when you think beyond where your locality. You do not need to travel around the world to make an impact on it neither do you need to have a branch of the business you intend to establish to be successful. You only need to have a mind that is larger than the sphere you currently reside; you can affect the world from any location you may be in the world. Since business initiatives and ideas find a way to leverage the internet to carry out their various activities, you can impact the world through this.

> *"All the world's a stage and all the men and women are merely players"* so says, William Shakespeare.

Multiply your influence:

For everyone that comes your way, find ways to meet a need in their lives. I've come to realise that impact can be defined in two words – **Meeting Needs.** When you touch a heart, you create a story which can be told over and over and in different places.

Be part of global initiatives:

In the year 2000, the United Nations (UN) formulated the Millennium Development Goals. The goals were meant to address the problem of poverty–hunger, shelter amongst others in many ways. Some of the goals were to eradicate extreme hunger and poverty, achieve universal primary education, improve maternal health, and combat HIV/AIDS, amongst others. As at 2015 –the time of expiry of these goals, statistics show that over 21 million lives were saved due to the various efforts put in by individuals, government agencies and Non-profit organisations. People from the highest positions of power and those at the grass-root level rose up to meet some of these goals. It was the coordinated and joint action of top decision makers and everyone at the lower levels to implement this kind of change. In several countries of the world, Nigeria inclusive, several young graduates served as volunteers for the MDG and helped to carry out individual projects and orientation exercises within their localities. These efforts added up to the overall success of the MDG.

Now how does this come into play?

You may not be able to start a global initiative, but you can choose to be a part of one. In 2015, the UN formulated the SDGs- Sustainable Development Goals which is an improvement upon previous goals set. You can choose to volunteer your time for any NGO of your choice. Be part of global initiatives that can affect the lives of others positively.

Thinking globally and acting begins by understanding that everyone is important and can be reached to make an impact in their lives. When it comes to wealth creation, it requires deep learning. The great and famous writer, Napoleon Hill who was the pioneer of the scientific approach to wealth creation and personal achievement, learned his wisdom from Andrew Carnegie whom he studied for over 20 years. During these years, he picked up insightful principles and knowledge that he contained in different books which have blessed the world. Through his choice to understudy Carnegie, he wrote great books. Some of these titles include Think and Grow Rich, Laws of Success.

Questions:

1. What stereotypes are limiting you from relating with certain people?

2. How well you treat others is a reflection of who you are. Draw a list of some of the perceptions you have about life – money, relationships, business, governance, politics and every other area of life. Now, look at them deeply, identify the ones that are empowering and those which are not. Begin to take conscious steps to renew your mind in those areas.

3. Find a cause you can volunteer for or a mentor that you can serve to learn wisdom from. You never know, you may be the one the world is waiting for.

CHAPTER SEVEN

Affect Humanity

"I want you to be concerned about your next door neighbour. Do you know your next door neighbour?"

-Mother Theresa

Ever wondered how little children in need of food for survival can smile and keep hope alive amidst death pangs, crumbled buildings, marred and scarred bodies? Certainly, you must have had your ears and eyes filled with news about nations hit by earthquakes, tsunamis or those in the throes of war. The world is filled with life threatening problems and much of it is caused by the activities of man. The inequality in the world is quite alarming. While one nation wastes tonnes of food, another nation thousands of miles away has men, women and children that starve to death. Some others live on with no chance of survival. While one nation experiences relative peace, another nation just across the border experiences war, famines, terrorism. Their people flee in millions to find refuge in other nations. It is to these kinds of people and situations that compassionate people are drawn.

Being a man of purpose, I often find myself constantly thinking of ways to solve problems in my environment. This is what drove my passion to start CodeSpark Foundation- an NGO whose primary aim is to reduce the level of computer science illiteracy in Nigeria. Sometimes people ask me these questions, why do you do all you do? What do you stand to gain by impacting lives at the expense of your time and resources? Well, my answer to them is PURPOSE. I strongly believe that everyone has a purpose and until it is discovered, you have not started living. I live for a purpose, I live for impact and I live to give my all to the very reason for which I've been created. I live to do good anytime, anywhere and anyhow. I have never known mediocrity; I am an influencer.

Wealthy people affect the world with their wealth. While you don't need to be a billionaire to affect humanity, having enough money helps to do more. The desire to affect the lives of people for good is philanthropy. A great leader, Myles Munroe once said, "When the purpose of a thing is not known, abuse is inevitable." This is the case with some celebrities who rose to prominence without understanding the purpose of wealth. No wonder some of them end up getting addicted to drugs.

How Charity changed Tony Robbins' life

According to the United Nations Food and Agricultural Organization, about 795 million people of 7.3 billion people on earth suffer chronic undernourishment–that's another word for hunger or food deprivation. We tend to dismiss statistics as numbers, but these are not just numbers, they are people who lack basic necessities of life. Tony Robbins fell into this category several years ago. Growing up, he had to knock on neighbours' doors to get food for himself and his siblings. One Thanksgiving day, there was a little knock on the door. Since his father had always told him that "No one cared about others", he did not expect the shock he got. Right there at the door was a man with a bag full of food that settled a befitting dinner for that night. In that moment, Tony decided that he would find a way to do the same –to feed the hungry and help those who were in need. Tony, through his charitable initiatives, feeds over 2 million people across the world yearly. That young boy grew to become a leading life coach, founder of 13 companies and consultant to several notable personalities in the world.

Charity sure can change a life.

So, what is it anyway?

Philanthropy is the desire to promote the welfare of others expressed especially by the generous donation of money to good causes. The word philanthropy is a combination of two words which can be traced back to the Greek words: *Philos* and *Anthropos*; which means Love and man. Putting these words together, philanthropy means love for mankind or humanity. For anyone who gives to others, it not only reveals a generous spirit but also a love for humanity.

One of the richest people to lead the way in philanthropy was Andrew Carnegie. He was quoted to have said, *"No man himself can become rich without enriching others."*

> *Philanthropy is the desire to promote the welfare of others expressed especially by the generous donation of money to good causes.*

Today, it is no surprise that 40 out of the top 50 philanthropists in the world are on the Forbes Billionaire list. There seems to be a culture of giving amongst those who become wealthy. Giving does not begin with substance, it begins with a heart. Those who are great givers always have a love for people and a desire to help others in some way. Businesses also begin with this same principle, howbeit for profit. When a business starts, it is usually to render a form of service or introduce a product to the marketplace. This same mindset follows charitable works. Several of the world's billionaires have pledged their fortune to be given in their lifetime and after their death.

> *Those who are great givers always have a love for people and a desire to help others in some way.*

Bill and Melinda Gates through their foundation have both given out over $24 billion as part of their charitable efforts. Warren Buffet of Omaha

Corporation has given out over $21 billion to charitable efforts pledging, even more, to be given in the coming years. Warren also committed his entire Berkshire Hathaway worth $58 billion which he says will be donated before or at his death. Mark and Priscilla his wife began the Chan Zuckerberg initiative whose aim is to *"advance human potential and promote equality in areas such as health, education, scientific research and energy."* They have invested $1 billion towards the success of this effort. As a matter of fact, they have pledged 99% of their Facebook shares worth $45 billion dollars to this initiative.

It doesn't stop with them. It appears to be a norm for most large corporations or businesses to have foundations where they disburse funds to meet a particular need in people's lives. It is in this same spirit that businesses carry out charitable deeds through Corporate Social Responsibility.

How can you adopt a philanthropic mindset?

It starts with a heart for people:

You do not need to have a billion dollars to affect the life of someone else; only have the heart for people. Realise that while there are people who may be doing better than you are, there are people who are doing worse. In Nigeria, there are countless streets and roads where little children are sent to beg. The only assurance that they will have a meal in a day is determined by the benevolence of people they meet on a daily basis. The ability to have compassion and reach out is the beginning point. Your heart for people is what will make you turn your "five loaves and two fish" into thousands to feed others. Simply taking a walk across the streets or watching the news on TV should stir up a desire within you to help others. Needs are everywhere.

Appreciate the much that you have:

Mahatma Gandhi, the Indian revolutionary leader, once said, *"The world has enough for everyone's need, but not enough for everyone's greed."* How true! If we all chose to live with contentment, we will begin to appreciate that which we do have. Those who became wealthy chose to become grateful not because they had everything when they first started, but because they recognised the value of whatever they had back then and today that has become a lifestyle.

You need not wait until you win a lottery to appreciate the beautiful things of life- every single day you wake up and can breathe again calls for happiness and gratitude.

> *You need not wait until you win a lottery to appreciate the beautiful things of life- every single day you wake up and can breathe again calls for happiness and gratitude.*

Life is too short to live always in anticipation. On the way to achieving your goals, appreciate how far you have come and been grateful for that which you do have. When you appreciate the much that you have, you will realise that you have at least a little to help others with. The thing about greed is that it blinds us from the abundance that surrounds us and creates a coveting attitude. Cultivate an attitude of gratitude.

See life through the lenses of others:

Imagine this for a second. You slept as a free man, but woke up in a Cell the next day (in another body) and learned from other prisoners that you were convicted of murder or some heinous crime. How would you feel if you found yourself in the body of a 65-year-old woman diagnosed with cancer with only 3 months to live? How about being involved in a ghastly accident and not been able to walk for life? These are real issues people grapple with today. When you visit the hospitals, there are legs hung up and several other people suffering from ailments that may end their lives. When you see life through the lenses of others, you will have compassion and the drive to be of help to others will suddenly arise. Are you so into yourself that you do not see the need to help others?

The more you have, the more you give. Most importantly, it is not in the largeness of the gift, but in the largeness of the heart, that philanthropy comes from.

The goal of life is to live full and to die empty.

Questions:

1. Pick up a pen and paper. Write down at least three (3) world problems you would solve with your wealth.

2. Start giving today. The secret to living is giving. Start with what you have. Realise how blessed you are and find something to give to someone around you. It may just make a world of difference to them.

3. Document all the experiences where you have been given a gift or a present and also document all your active donations and gifts to others. Reading this will make you realise the beauty of being both a receiver and a giver.

REFERENCES

❖ https://www.weforum.org/agenda/201
7/04/the-myth-of-the-successful-
college-
dropout?utm_content=buffer18c3d&ut
m_medium=social&utm_source=facebo
ok.com&utm_campaign=buffer
(Accessed June, 2017).

❖ Pastor Sunday Adelaja's blog
http://sundayadelajablog.com/5905-2/
(Accessed June, 2017).

❖ http://ethanbeute.com/forbes-400-
rich-american-education-level-college-
dropout/ (Accessed June, 2017).

❖ Pastor Sunday Adelaja's blog
http://sundayadelajablog.com/visual-
step-step-process-elon-musk-built-
multi-billion-dollar-empire/ (Accessed
June, 2017).

ABOUT THE AUTHOR

Olaniyi Ayeni is a National Reformer, Motivational Speaker, IT Consultant, Writer, and Orator. He loves encouraging people to lead a better life, most especially young minds of all race and faith.

He is an element of change, a catalyst for innovation, a dictator of peace, an agent of progress, a lover of God and all His beautiful creation. He is currently the founder of CodeSpark Nigeria an NGO focused on teaching kids how to code and exposing them to the world of technology and innovation.

You can connect with him on Facebook

Twitter: @olaniyi_king
Facebook: facebook.com/TheOlaniyiAyeni

Instagram: @olaniyiking

Website: olaniyiking.com

Email: hello@Olaniyiking.com

23837807R00115

Printed in Great Britain
by Amazon